W0082568

Praise for
Conquering Tomorrow Today: Six Exemplar Lives

"Readable and inspiring"

"This book is not only readable and inspiring, it has the energy one expects from Bruce Piasecki, an author with a sharp wit, deep learning, and a broad perspective on the world. He's a writer I always read with pleasure."

—Jay Parini

Best-selling author of *The Last Station*

"A force for healing"

"At a fractious moment, when the coronavirus global pandemic is decimating our economic and social life, Bruce Piasecki's new book can be a force for healing and understanding. Piasecki writes in a compelling style. He offers clear-eyed portraits of successful and compassionate people, as we have seen before in Emerson, Freud, and Churchill. These profiles offer the immediacy of oral history, the hard-won knowledge of lived experience, and authentic voices that will draw readers in. You will end up admiring these people, and Piasecki. You can take to heart the wisdom they impart about the storms of today and tomorrow."

—Paul Grondahl

Journalist, author, and Director of
The New York State Writers Institute at the University at Albany

---

"Deeply Consequential"

"Capitalism is most often these days rapacious, self-serving, and a generator of inequality. Yet there are leaders in our capitalist world who know better and do better. Bruce Piasecki has met a few of them. The six leaders profiled in these pages are deeply consequential, note here what Piasecki calls social response capitalism as a force at play in a tightly global world"

—Sandy Schram

Professor of Political Science, Hunter College

"Brilliantly portrayed"

"Effective leaders go about their business somewhat differently than their peers. That's the magic in these case studies by Bruce Piasecki. Their differences, brilliantly portrayed, allow them to achieve results that others can only imagine. This is invigorating stuff. This book is rich with 'fun-to-know' stuff."

—Tim Lindsey

President and CEO, Highlander Innovation

"Deeply surprising"

"Most business leaders that we know are larger-than-life characters. That is what's so deeply surprising about this new book by Bruce Piasecki. What he explores is how modest, quietly spoken effective people can have as significant an impact as some of their gregarious counterparts. Many can learn from those that dare."

—Richard Ellis

Vice President, Corporate Social Responsibility,

Walgreens Boots Alliance

"Worthy for your tomorrow"

"Aristotle notes that role models are crucial for developing virtues. Bruce Piasecki's compelling descriptions of "Six that Make a Difference" dramatize models of virtuous leadership for our age where mastering the complexity of everyday requires unprecedented collaborative skills. Read this book. It will prove worthy for your tomorrow."

—William M. Throop

Professor of Philosophy and Environmental Studies,

Green Mountain College

The Social Intelligence of
LINDA COADY

Other Books by Bruce Piasecki

America's Future in Toxic Waste Management

Beyond Dumping

Corporate Environmental Strategy

Doing More With Less

Doing More With Teams

Environmental Management and Business Strategy

In Search of Environmental Excellence

Missing Persons: A Memoir

New World Companies

Stray Prayers

The Surprising Solution

World, Inc.

The Social Intelligence of
LINDA COADY

BRUCE PIASECKI

An advance book excerpt from
Conquering Tomorrow Today: Six Exemplar Lives

Creative Force Fund
2020

The Social Intelligence of Linda Coady
by Bruce Piasecki

First published in 2020 by
Creative Force Fund
158 Stone Church Road
Ballston Spa, NY 12020

www.ahcgroup.com

Copyright © 2020 by Bruce Piasecki

ALL RIGHTS RESERVED. No part of this publication may be reproduced,
scanned, uploaded, stored in a retrieval system, or transmitted, in any
form or by any means, electronic, mechanical, photocopying, recording,
or otherwise, without the prior written permission of the publisher,
except in the case of brief quotations embodied in critical reviews and
certain other noncommercial uses permitted by copyright law.

ISBN (Print): 978-1-09833-937-1
ISBN (eBook): 978-1-09833-938-8

Printed and distributed by BookBaby
www.bookbaby.com

Printed in the United State of America

10   9   8   7   6   5   4   3   2   1

Table of Contents

Foreword by Chris Coulter, CEO, GlobeScan........................ 1

Case Study: The Life of Linda Coady 7

Chapter Snapshot: Linda Coady... 38

Afterword by Darryl Poole... 39

Reflections on Personality and Social Cohesion 43

Full Book Table of Contents... 47

The Conversation: About Bruce Piasecki............................. 48

Foreword
by
Chris Coulter, CEO, GlobeScan

I am glad I got to see this book before you in its early stages. I attended some of Bruce Piasecki's workshops as he was developing this book, and met through the years several of those featured in this collection of smart profiles.

As we enter this third decade of the new millennium, it is clear that we are swimming in unchartered waters. That is why Piasecki calls this, in his classic 2007 book, a "swift and severe world." You see the sample book case study here on Eileen Fisher.

Every facet of our life—from the economy to politics to the natural environment—has become more volatile, uncertain, complex, and ambiguous. Some call this complex "the age of VUCA." Piasecki calls this an age of mistrust, mischief, and turmoil. This book examines how to get past this age.

Life has become *more volatile*, because interests are shifting across the world, accelerated by technology and new geopolitics; *more uncertain*, because of shifting societal expectations, mass inequality, and the impacts of climate change; *more complex*, because of the growing interdependence of the economy, society, and the environment in a global world; and *more ambiguous*, because our traditional governance and power structures are unfit for this new age.

At GlobeScan, we study these social shifts in world view from our offices in Brazil, Canada, Europe, Singapore, and elsewhere, tabulating billions of inputs. Strangely enough, Bruce Piasecki's findings echo these larger trends from his personal observations of world views and the behavior of firms. Yet, while underlining the importance of our findings, he also gives us a way up and out into the 21st century. His trends diagnostic is presented as solutions, and paths of discovery.

We have faced other significant challenges throughout history, from war to political scandal to economic calamity, and more often than not, have found our way through them.

When times are difficult, we have looked to that uniquely human property to help us navigate our way through disruption: leadership.

Enlightened, Inspired, and Thoughtful Leadership

This is a precious resource which we must cultivate and encourage, as it has the potential to mobilize solutions to create a better future. It is in this context that I am so grateful for Bruce Piasecki's important book.

The timeliness of this book is in helping us learn from remarkable leaders and finding ways to apply their insights and experiences to many aspects of our lives, so we all become better and more effective leaders.

Notice this book's scope: "How Wisdom Survives Chaos." I find this aptly captures the urgency of better leadership to build consensus and trust. We need these six types of leaders and their bold actions to get us to the future we want. In this age of polarization and declining trust in institutions, we need leaders who can help our societies heal and work together to tackle the extraordinary challenges before us. These exemplar lives do exactly that, case by case.

The six people featured in Bruce's book—Linda Coady, Eileen Fisher, Frank Loy, Jack Robinson, John Streur, and Steve Percy—provide powerful, even colorful, profiles of leadership. I have had the honor and good fortune to have meet some of these remarkable individuals and have followed their careers. In Bruce Piasecki's hands, these met individuals come alive for many, as they should.

These six come from very different walks of life. They represent a diverse array of sector experience, including government, energy, fashion, and finance. Yet, as you will see as you devour this book, they all share a passion for embracing complexity and leading with purpose. Further, they all have demonstrated the power of that indispensable leadership quality: *listening*.

These remarkable six individuals have repeatedly shown *the value of deep listening*, engagement, and patient consensus-building to effect real change. As Piasecki shows with wit and historic insights, we have a great deal to learn from them in this anxious age of turmoil and distrust.

Here at GlobeScan, I have a privileged vantage point through my work to see how expectations of stakeholders and the general public across the world are shifting in response to all of the challenges we face. By happy circumstance, GlobeScan has worked for years for some of Bruce Piasecki's global management consulting clients. We do the empirical work; Piasecki and his team of lawyers and former executives refine the strategy once inside a given firm like Merck or Toyota or Walgreens.

While there is growing dissatisfaction with the status quo and heightening anxiety to the environmental crisis unfolding around us, especially among young people, *there is also a deep thirst for new approaches* in the way we live, work, consume, produce and collaborate.

Relating This Book to the Rest of Our World

As we look into the next decades, it is critical that corporations shape their strategies and public responses in fulfillment of the United Nation's Sustainable Development Goals in 2030. These 17 goals (with a total of 169 targets) were developed collectively by governments, civil society, and business and represent the best definition of the future we all want. They cover aspirational goals such as the end of poverty and hunger, access to proper education and health care, gender equity, and much more.

Together, they represent an integrated and renewed approach to how we can live, work and play. At times these seem overwhelming; yet, in the hands of this gifted writer, they are made more intelligible through the lives of the six studied by Piasecki.

With all this in mind, this is a timely book for our age.

It mixes all the best of Bruce's instincts and experience—knowing the key issues of our day and the stakes involved; having a keen understanding and appreciation of the historical context; and showcasing, with a generous spirit, the lives of leaders that can teach us a better way forward.

Some of the critical answers for the new leadership lie within the experiences and stories of these special six. We are all better for having their lives so wonderfully and enthusiastically documented by Bruce Piasecki.

I will end with a few lines from the book itself, as I think they perfectly set us up for learning about Linda, Eileen, Frank, Jack, John, and Steve. Piasecki notes:

"Back in the 19th century, when there were so fewer people, great thinkers thought about what is humankind's role in changing the face of the earth. Now a mere 200 years later, we ask what is humankind's role in making this humanized planet sustainable."

Come meet this wonderful set of people.

Chris Coulter
CEO, GlobeScan
Canada, Brazil, United States, Singapore

Case Study:
The Life of Linda Coady

Staging an Olympics is a big deal. You attract thousands of the world's elite athletes, their entourages, as well as 40 to 60 corporate sponsors and hundreds of suppliers. It is a grand show, where millions of people watch what you've done on TV, as hundreds of thousands attend your event. You find yourself helping set a world stage as never before.

The life of Linda Coady gives us an insider account of what it is like. What matters is not what she actually did to attract First Nations, a wide stretch of construction workers, a network of corporate providers. What matters is the manner in which she accomplished this, so the reader can take this example and "become like Linda" in other large complex public settings in this age of climate and carbon constraints.

Each modern Olympics involves building a moderate-size city within an old city—structures to house athletes safely, more than a dozen stadiums, new train lines, better roads, new food stalls, and more. "You buy and need practically everything," a Canadian health official told me, "even enough Clorox disinfecting wipes to go around our globe several times."

How does this relate to your world today? As I write this, there is a real chance that the 2020 Tokyo Olympics will be cancelled or delayed due to the outbreak of the coronavirus. The National

Basketball Association season has been cancelled, as has the 248-year-old St. Patrick's Day parade in Manhattan. My daughter's medical school, one among thousands, has been closed for remote, computer-based learning. People who are involved in Olympics think about these kinds of risks that prove comprehensive. Though most of us like to avoid thinking about it, risk is a human experience. Those that know how to proceed and advance through risk make the future we all enjoy, or dread.

The Facts, and the Fancy

As I strove to display in my book, *Doing More with Teams*, modern sport is where the world of risk, competitive inclusiveness, and creativity in marketing join hands. This world attracts some of the best paid advance thinkers. Linda Coady is one of the more cleverly enduring.

For five years, Linda Coady was the Sustainability executive for the 2010 Winter Olympics in Vancouver. For many people, this would be the culmination of a career. But for Linda, this was a mid-life beginning, one that would give her new perspective about the nature of people, and one she would later use to try and move giant firms and address massive social needs for food, climate, and land.

Days at Home, Days Before College

But to more fully understand Linda, we must start much earlier, during her youthful days before college. The first time I asked Linda about her beginnings, *she mentioned that she came from two worlds: one of science and social leadership, and one of faith and virtues.*

In this case, I will argue that it is rare to be able to straddle successfully these two realms. It is easier for any capitalist, any modern leader, to lean in on the science part, the social leadership part. And very hard for them to embrace publicly the faith and virtue components evident in their work. It is as if C.S. Lewis's famous reflection about how there are "two cultures" in the world has been forgotten, as we favor the world of science over the reality that many need to believe in a few things as more important than fact, things like community, faith, a distant future.

What do we mean by two worlds? In order for folks to reassemble in groups, the very essence of social intelligence, folks will need to get past fears of The Virus. Thinking about today itself, in mid-March 2020, one is tempted to ask if there is enough Clorox in the world to satisfy this new range of risks. I think corporates can always supply enough at the right price. But will there prove to be enough people Linda Coady?

Since I began writing about sports in earnest ten years back, you can watch how stadiums deal with and eliminate most of the threats of staph, e. coli, salmonella, strep, or kleb from a scientific point of view. But what about coronavirus? What about the fear that comes with it? This week the National Basketball Association terminated the entire rest of the season. My daughter's medical school was one of hundreds that asked their students not to come back after Spring break. This is true March Madness, a time of disruption to the world economy.

I believe this world of panic and resolve will be more global and more common for the rest of my life. That is why deep listening matters.

I bring us back to Linda Coady, because by chance she has done this kind of work, deep listening, most of her life. Linda Coady, like Frank Loy, resisted my attempts to write about her life several times, asking that I not compare her listening to the quiet we see in Rembrandt's Christ.

She wrote me in reply to an earlier draft: "For the record, I was raised a Catholic because my parents were religious. But I haven't practiced Catholicism since I was at University.... I have always a been a city girl. My parents lived in a suburb of Vancouver with a backyard the size of a postage stamp. You could reach out and touch the house next door. Our house was less than 20 minutes from the office towers of downtown Vancouver—Canada's third largest city." You see in this prose a desire to state facts; yet what matters is how she frames those facts.

As I spent four years digging into what people say about Linda's quietude, I am convinced that this city girl with a prominent doctor as her father was destined to work on major social challenges. When we think about how hard it is to think through the flattery and the fakery involved in big time sports, the politics of deception in corporate life, and the great fatigue of misfortune in government work, you see why this book, and in particular this section on Linda Coady, really is a social reflection on what works and what does not in this swift and severe modern world.

At the end of this case you might conclude: Why we lie is because we must; it is a part of human nature to frame resolutions to move forward in a complex world. Why we need folks like Linda Coady to assemble groups will become clear in this book. For now, let's return to what made this big-city girl see a bigger world, a world divided.

Coming Back to Linda's Beginnings

The next time—about three years ago now—that I asked Linda Coady about her origins, she answered with much more detail and nuance and insight than at first, but the essence was the same. She learned a great deal by the great differences between her father, mother, and siblings.

By the tenth interview, it was natural that *we'd explore this duality of faith and science* every time we spoke. It does not matter that she thinks herself now a lapsed Catholic. She emanates a world view that unites faith in people and facts about what society needs.

As Linda spoke in my company settings, and during our private conversations across years, I kept two columns going in my notes as she spoke: one column on the techniques that will work in a science-based technological world; and the hidden column on what she was revealing about faith and virtue. In my reading of her life, she has led a life that disrobes fakery, an exciting life *that helps groups surge forward with facts and faith*, with social purpose and the common good in mind.

The science world came from her father. He was a medical doctor, a pathologist, "and pioneer in laboratory medicine" in British Columbia. They lived in a suburb of Vancouver, where Dr. Campbell Coady headed the hospital laboratory. He also had time to establish a success-ful private practice. She adds:

> *My father established a chain of medical laboratories that served several cities and suburbs of Vancouver and the greater Vancouver area. The population of the area served by my father was 1.5 million citizens in his day. That now currently has surged to over 2.5 million.*

Over dinner conversations, she absorbed from her father a sense of respect, social inclusion, and professionalism. The hidden wealth of some doctors can be seen in how much of society they come to know.

It is easy for me to pick up on the social significance of her father in her eventual jobs. For a doctor listens hard, far more than professors, bankers, or even police. Think this through for a minute. As I watch my daughter become a doctor, and as I reflect how I went into business rapidly after dropping out of pre-medical training at Cornell, it was because of my lack of ability to listen long and hard. How doctors treat their particular spectrum of humanity with attention to detail is what Linda Coady has come to embody. It is a direct lineage from father to daughter:

- Listen.
- Be careful.
- Be attentive.
- Be kind.
- Solve real problems.

The Russian doctor Anton Chekov wrote many plays that dramatize these points, as does the life story of the great New Jersey doctor and poet William Carlos Williams. If trained as a doctor, who is attentive to the human details of drama (for what is sickness but a moment of drama?), you listen when you can, and deeply. Sure, all doctors have tons of data, reams of materials that show blood does not lie. But how a patient presents that self is the matter at hand. How a doctor hears what that patient presents is often the difference between life and death.

Linda Coady's mother kept order in a house of four children; and "was intelligent on how to navigate the world." Here Linda meant her mom had the touch of pragmatism that complemented the far more generous persona her father had to assume. Some readers would want me to say here that Linda's mother balanced a father whose main task was helping others in need, as her mother taught her how to take care of herself. But that would be too simple. In talking with others about how Linda presents the dynamics of her youthful home, both from her husband and from others who have known Linda in multiple settings, I do not believe it was that simple, that conventional. Both parents were extremely intelligent and effective. What matters in this case is how they taught her to navigate a world where there are believers and scientists and engineers.

Thinking about this mother–father dynamic, I think we can infer a few attributes about Linda Coady. The love of science often takes a firm, stubborn sense of initial order—how things should be. Yet, in writing my Memoir while meeting Linda Coady, I reflected a great deal on family life. Family life can be both orderly and disorderly at the same time. It requires pragmatism of a different sort. You get from Linda's reflections of her days at her birth-home, and from the tactics she employs in her work, that she has come to embrace and inhabit these different attributes. This adds some insight past any norms in a conventional parent–daughter/daughter–"rest of family group" dynamics.

By the fourth year observing Linda, I got the strong impression that her two sisters and her brother were quite different from each other; and that Linda relished the real range of their personalities. Her younger sister teaches now at a Catholic school. Her brother died at an early age from complications of juvenile diabetes. The first time Linda mentioned her brother, she said, "Well, he is in an entirely different place now." I find that fascinating, as she worked consistently to ask me to "just state the facts about my brother, that would be more respectful." Her younger sister is a computer science professor at one of Canada's major universities. All this readied Linda Coady to celebrate diversity.

In fact, one of her favorite focus phrases that fell from my mouth once in a group setting was: "competitive yet inclusive." That is what Linda goes for, allowing people to compete for their positions, yet be inclusive of differences in the art of getting to a common goal. I was speaking to about 60 clients at once, and I described my basketball coach as "competitive yet inclusive." She said afterward at dinner, "Bingo. That sums it up, Bruce."

As I did not meet her siblings, it would be wrong to extrapolate further; but from discussions with Linda's lifelong husband, you can see Linda "enjoys the range of personalities in her family." In like manner, you can see she enjoys the range of leaders we assemble in a typical Corporate Affiliates workshop, where I can always count on Linda "hearing it all, all the nuance, all the wow moments and phrasings."

An Early Example That Technical Excellence Is Limiting

Without saying it, when Linda Coady was selected by Enbridge to become their top executive dealing with the external world, she was the odd woman out. Neither engineer nor scientist in a firm awash with technical talent, she was a people person, a person who knew early in life that technical excellence is limiting.

Let me demonstrate this in my own life, so the readers can relax into why this is important for the future. The first university where I got tenure, Clarkson University (Potsdam, New York, a few miles from Canada and the greater Ottawa complex), the god on campus was engineering.

It is not an exaggeration that those that worshipped in the halls of engineering were deeply respected, and those that were not engineers did not earn much deep listening. Clarkson is an excellent engineering school, a rural school up near the Canadian border in the northern kingdom of what is still referred to as the North Country of New York. When the reigning President of Clarkson invited me and my wife to the tenure dinner with his wife and children, it turns out that all seven family members were engineers! My wife and I looked at each other, and held our tongues. As soon as my wife and I reached home near the great Adirondack Raquette river, we said: "We have to get out of this place!" We were used to libraries and museums. We were used to press debates and great books, not an engineer's laconic type of precision. You will see this developed in the Steve Percy chapter, where we watch an RPI engineer become a world executive.

How does this relate to the worlds of Linda Coady? Well, some say that money makes the world go around; and some even say that the best engineers come to understand the disciplines of finance. But how many of them pause much to understand people?

This book argues that people who understand people make the world go round. Their wisdom survives the chaos of more data, more drawings, more technothink.

I think it simply significant that Linda Coady had a doctor and a pragmatist as her parents, rather than a household with two generations of engineers. More on this later, since entering into Enbridge, one is entering an engineering culture, much like those I've felt consulting for Raytheon, or teaching my M.S. students to take good jobs at United Technologies, Lockheed Martin, and our new world companies like Apple, Microsoft, and the like.

I mention this because Linda has always been interested in how groups cohere; where "group think" comes from; and why there is a fair amount of comfortable fakery in technical certainties and legal positioning. This may be one of the key attributes of success—people who understand people, and their range of competencies. This conclusion I derive from having met several of her staff through the years, and from being a management advisor to some of them after she retires from Enbridge: they all come in the end to talk about Linda's special skills at discerning higher facts, the things of faith that people can hold onto.

A Strong Father Mixes with an Order of Teaching Nuns

In the Frank Loy case we note a rare skill: his ability to respect technical and humanistic needs and competencies. That is the genius in most diplomats in a nutshell, and what enables some to level off as technical VPs and others to reach the top slots at firms.

From the start, Linda said the second major influence in her life were the nuns with the Sisters of Charity of St. Louis. They were a teaching Order of Nuns who ran the catholic girl's school that first formed Linda Coady. It was in range from 48 to 78 girls, where Linda Coady studied from 8th grade (when it first opened) through the 12th grade. The school keep meticulous notes, always trying to rein in the maliciousness in girls while supporting their altruistic potential and potencies. Her memories of this place remain, even after more than 40 years, vivid, extended, and fascinating. I find this true when I interviewed the last 100 executive success stories. They remember the turning points of youth vividly. Linda knew from the start that "the nuns hoped the best students would join the Sisterhood." Outsmarting the weight of that early expectation took early skills, I presumed, and Linda agreed.

"Here," she told me, "is where I realized things are not black and white, *that fundamental human traits are discernible.* The nuns emphasized the virtues over the vices. Here we were trained in humility, inclusion, and what excellence might be." This may be the most important thing she told me through the years about herself.

I placed emphasis here on her phrase "that fundamental human traits are discernible." If we jump ahead two decades to her executive work, she was known by the leaders at Enbridge for her "*spectrum maps*: records of the fundamental human traits of the thousands of stakeholders Enbridge had to address to satisfy the requirements of receiving a permit at one of their massive pipelines crossing many jurisdictions" (a direct quote from someone who admired her on staff at Enbridge). Others spoke about executives calling her at night or on weekends to collect "Linda's view" of some matter in the wind that hinged on a human balance point—not another matter of technology and markets.

I suggested to her, in our sixth interview, that the mix of these early homegrown human traits, rendered by her in modern corporate language, might in the past be called "fortitude and care."

She agreed instantly, and added, "But I also learned something about the vices—*the vice of intolerance, the dangers in arrogance, the powerful distractions in adhering to the preoccupations with the self.*" This active synthesis of Mom and Dad's worlds made her ready for a world of disinformation, lying, and basic self-interest. Even a teaching nun wanted her to be a teaching nun.

"But," she reflected, "the greatest virtue the overall experience helped me adopt, both from my father and from the Catholic high school, was *that to do my best requires focus. There is a fundamental human virtue in focus*, the cultivated ability to bear down." The ability to bear down becomes a honed skill in her life after high school.

It was in her last three paragraphs of inputs that I decided I'd write about her rather than Michael Bloomberg. I had an offer to write for Amazon about Mr. Bloomberg. But if you think about it, the world needs more people like Linda Coady. Nothing against Michael Bloomberg—I would have voted for him. It is simply that these abilities to discern vice from virtue make the world go around.

Linda Coady is now 68, and she is about to accept a most prominent and difficult job from the Premier of Canada. Here is the point. Often, in the decade I've now observed Linda Coady directly, you can see her sit mostly still for two days in an important meeting, bearing down, listening deep. Then, after these pensive, almost meditative moments, she sums up—for all still alert in the room—"a recognition," a set of "focus phrases" (my phrase to my wife, like *I love you*), that are the best thoughts of practically everyone in the room. I have seen it several dozen times in our Affiliates workshops: the crowd nods in general agreement.

Extrapolating from Vancouver into the Greater Heritage of Italy

This March of 2020 I am deeply disturbed that the 61 million kindred souls in Italy that I love to visit are under containment. It seems like a science fiction novel to me, still. Yet this is real. When we do not listen to science, when we do not know how important faith in society really is, we get in a pickle that can kill us.

Now, if you think about how assembling people is needed, you must also think about eliminating the lies that distract and that distort. I have characterized this chapter that deals with faith and fact as "achieving social cohesion in a time of distrust and turmoil." You all can feel what I mean. Linda Coady worked through these matters while at home, with the Sisters, and in her early years. She came into the scene of Big Sports and Big Pipelines knowing the two worlds.

To dramatize this with more nuance, I want to have us reflect some on the glory that is Italy.

My experience in management consulting suggests that few people have the ability to quickly notice and combat incorrect stories about themselves and others in a group. Steve Percy has that skill in spades, as does Frank Loy in complex group settings requiring diplomatic resolution.

Although Linda Coady does not want me to put this higher set of skills into a discussion on "Why We Lie," I must. In order to appreciate the tremendous talent evident in these six that make a difference, we need to know more about why humans lie. This has to do more with the world we live in than with any of the six I am writing about. But at this point in the argument, Linda Coady becomes a good way to dramatize the skill set.

Linda writes: "I never spoke with you about why people lie. I do not base my life work on lying. It is simply wrong to bring that theme into what I do."

It is not that she is protesting too much, as in a Shakespeare master-work. It is that she'd rather have me only talk about the virtues of her approach. But please remember she has already told us a good deal about vices in the quotes about her schooling. In addition to the ability to underline higher facts, Linda has the ability to know when to navigate past group think, or group lying, or individual self-serving lies. As my firm enters its 40th year as a management consulting group, I find that my job is mostly to do the same: to pick winners and avoid lies.

It is too rough to simply call it "a good bullshit detector," as I've heard lawyers and engineers refer to this dose of suspicion. What is different from that detection is Linda's ability to make something of value to the group by discerning the vices. She spoke about the primary need for focus. I've watched her now, that silence, that listening: it filters out the bullshit, the idle bravado, the elements to which Frank Loy sensitizes us as unnecessary flamboyance.

The world is replete with one-sided stories taken and magnified. The world is full of idle wheel-spinning. Take it from me, I made real money as a Ph.D. student, as well as during the writing of my first book for Simon and Schuster in 1988–1990 by helping a key appropriations lobbying firm discern doable truths from Congressional lies. But Linda seems to have cultivated a set of higher facts even more than a lobbyist. She has a more time-tested, humane framework. She doesn't only count votes. She judges the vices and virtues of this world, which the group can relate to and then take action on. You need to recognize that this involves understanding why people lie.

You cannot make too much of this skill for the next decades of this century. Now to the glory of Italia part.

Perhaps you'd want to visit Giotto's famous paintings hanging in Padova, Italia, to contemplate the full extent of this important skill. Giotto depicts *Charity, Fortitude, Temperance*, and other virtues in the Cappella degli Scrovegni of his wealthy patron. And here he also paints the corresponding vices: *Envy, Inconstancy, Wrath*, etc.

Giotto: *Charity*   Giotto: *Temperance*

I can imagine (but have not talked with Linda about this) that she knows people who have defeated themselves through vices. Over time, our civilization has lost the nuances of some of these ancient insights into human traits; but for Linda Coady, *the attention to character nuance comes as second nature.* I believe this is what she means by "focus." She never lost this from teaching or from her parents at home, and listens for it continuously.

What Manifests a Calling?

I asked Linda how she found her "calling." She modestly joked, "I am still searching for that, a calling…." After a long, thoughtful pause, she added, "I found a direction, a pathway, anyway. I now think of one's calling as a lifelong journey, much like my subject—sustainable value—itself."

I later asked for further clarification, and she answered, to my surprise, by touching on issues of serendipity. *"You have to have faith and respect of when a turn comes your way. Right?"* Faith—respect—a-turn-your-way: now that was a unique set of combined and explosive phrases. I am more ready than ever to have you look at more great Italian or Dutch religious paintings!

I tried to dig deeper on this knowing phrase of hers, a "turn." I think it means when social history embraces your role in it. By the end of this book's case work on Jackie Robinson, you will see something similar and more nuanced. *Even if she does not consciously mean it, Linda leans back to a long spiritual tradition in framing a life journey as she does. She modestly says she is a lapsed Catholic.* That is not my point. The new generation needs the abilities to discern fact and faith, to distinguish what is doable from what is waste.

Her Story About Trees

British Columbia is a land of many trees, including some of the oldest northern rainforests in the world.

The province's history is full of colorful stories of big trees. I know the Dean of Management and Technology at the University of British Columbia, and he is an engineer in awe of big trees. Linda Coady wants you to remember this. She spent much of her early career with "big stories, big trees, big logs, and big lumberjacks." She actually sent me carefully crafted pages, as in a Memoir, about this part of her life.

Linda did much of her early work, before the Vancouver Olympics and Enbridge, working in the forest industry to advance new methods of forest conservation and sustainability management on the coast of British Columbia. "It was during a time that locals in BC often refer to as the 'War in the Woods'—when the province's logging practices were the focus of protests locally, and noted globally."

Linda does not know that I was writing a book called Earth As Hostage at this time she was up there. I had interviewed with the FBI's bureau of counterterrorism about her issues, and studied for the government actual bios of those that would eventually be arrested, but not successfully charged, in some of these protests, both in the States and in Canada. I never published my findings, since some of the terrorists pledged to burn down my home if I did. I tell my readers that now because Linda wants us to think this was all about good things, values and virtues over vice and destruction.

It was a war. And Linda was a key general in it. She was among those trying to end the conflict, and she had the unique distinction of working first on the company side of the table (for Weyerhaeuser and its predecessors), and then for the moderate environmentalists, the World Wildlife Fund Canada.

Meanwhile, I had sent a six-foot-six researcher from my firm to infiltrate one of the Earth First camps and rendezvous centers in Canada, the northern parts of the States, Canton, New York, and eventually where a key action took place against one of my firm's Corporate Affiliates—the Palo Alto Nuclear Plant outside Phoenix and owned by Arizona Public Service and a half dozen other legal entities. Linda is simply wrong in suggesting that this war was only about logging. My eventual client, Louisiana Pacific, took a good deal of the heat from the protestors up in her areas and ours, where some of their loggers were severely injured when metal spikes embedded in the old stands were causing chainsaws to back-jump and cut into the limbs of the workers. I took some of our photographs to the Hoover building in Washington, and did the same at the *Denver Post*, and in Canada in places I'd rather not name.

Linda describes in her retrospective memoir that one of the turning points in the conflict was centered on this: the moderate environmental groups and the forest companies had the power to stop the other from doing what it had to achieve. *Logging versus Protection* is one way to think of it.

Linda credits a brilliant facilitator who, whenever an impasse loomed, would exhort the industry and the environmentalists at the table with a call that admonished: "No wishful thinking. No self-pity. Be brutally honest in your assessment of what your choices really are."

Linda notes that from this "sometimes painful honesty emerged a diverse coalition of leaders from forest executives and environmentalists, Indigenous group leaders, workers, scientists, engineers, and government representatives." Over the years, this group of people co-developed a breakthrough plan for conservation and management that left intact the largest remaining tract of coastal temperate old growth forest in the world."

Like any negotiated plan, the coastal forest plan was complex, and far too technical for a book like this one in your hands.

What Linda wants my readers to know is this: "The process I experienced profoundly changed the dynamic of protest, when we realized that we did not need to agree on everything to proceed" (I should note that the spiking of old-growth trees by Earth First and others stopped as well). After anchoring the change in a few good solid first steps, many other social goods flowed from this, and a multimillion-dollar deal was agreed upon.

In this early battlefield, Linda had a front row seat on how social innovation and social cohesion works. She took these tools into the other parts of her life. It can all be summed up as follows:

- Listen
- Discern
- Solve

An Olympic Effort

Linda's years working as the head of Sustainability for the Vancouver Olympics taught her the value of listening to make judgments based on social inclusion. You can sense this best in her own words, reflecting back on those five years, spoken in our second of a dozen interviews:

> I had watched the Sydney Olympics in Australia and then the Winter Olympics in Norway start a popular trend of trying to reduce the environmental footprint of these massive undertakings. When the Organizing Committee of the Vancouver event reached out to me at the start of the planning, I saw a realm of real possibilities. That is what attracted me to leave my job at the World Wildlife Fund of Canada as a Vice President of the Pacific Region, where I grew up.

Sports is a lucrative industry with some very intelligent global business leaders beneath the actual games. Yet deeper still, Linda had a special way of framing it beyond sports. "I had done environmental non-governmental work for some time, and before that I had worked for giant Canadian forest products companies. Here was a chance to grow my knowledge of how society wants both sustainability and better communities at once."

She agreed to serve the Vancouver Olympic Organizing Committee at what turned out to be a new advance on the prior efforts to lessen impact. "I saw this group of leaders, and key sponsors like Bell Canada and RONA (later bought by Lowe's Home Improvement), wanting to extend the trends from Sydney into a social spectrum of concerns. A key issue was the inclusion of communities that do not normally gain access to elite sports events, from inner city communities to single urban Moms groups." Linda headed up those efforts by the sponsors to ensure groups like these were included in the benefits created by the games.

Once again, the magic is in her phrasing, her thinking:

> The trick to success in this social setting was to involve new groups in the mix of the giants, so we worked to involve the four key First Nations (among dozens) up front in joint training benefits and programs. This way, we joined the benefits of a global sporting event with those in need. They worked to provide training and employment in areas like carpentry and other trade skills.

Later, both Bell Canada and RONA would praise Linda's efforts at helping the corporate sponsors learn things they never thought about in both community relations and supply chain innovation. "There were ticket programs for the underprivileged, free access for some, and plenty of civics for all." As she was including the community to this elite sporting event, she was also changing the way the corporates think about their real range of customers. This extended what many now call the *Corporate Social Responsibility* of the firm.

Yet Linda took it further: "These programs also provided some glue between the governments' interests in expanding opportunities for training and the corporate needs, as the city of Vancouver aligned on these programs and initiatives with the regional governments and the Federal government of Canada." In characteristic humility, Linda then said: "This is now a common practice in large complex development projects in Canada." It was some heavy lifting that she made seem light.

Linda listens with passion to focus a group.

She notes, "I saw the Olympics as a bigger pathway to the social dimensions of sustainability, a way to step out and step up, a pathway to frame more robust and better integrated efforts that both lessen environmental impact and focus on the creation of social value."

Accepting a Large Corporate Job at Enbridge

After what she learned working the Olympics, Linda saw an opportunity and larger challenge in bringing her ideas of social cohesion to a giant firm in North America. The giant she chose is one that many would not think would be interested in her approach, due to the nature of their work: massive energy infrastructure projects.

Linda worked, with a staff of up to 14, as head of sustainability at Enbridge, one of the world's largest pipeline companies. Here she took on nearly a decade of the most heated debates in Canada over energy development and transport, involving the siting of pipelines and the complex tax policies of energy competitiveness. She led the team on Enbridge's public disclosures on social, environmental, and governance issues, orchestrated their stakeholder meetings, coordinated communications with government officials, and led a very active life with peer giants in Canada and other large companies feeling the pinch of climate change.

This also involved moving her family to Calgary, Enbridge's home. Vastly different in landscape and culture from her home in the Pacific Northwest with its sparkling city of Vancouver, Calgary is the new 21st-century Houston or Dallas..

There are great reserves of oil up there, along with massive reserves of minerals for mining giants. You can think of this as a boom town of global consequence. Giant companies like Agrium, the world's second largest fertilizer manufacturer, and Suncor Energy, the largest developer of the oil sands, are headquartered in Calgary. Calgary is strongly pro-business—and very different in feel and politics from progressive Vancouver.

When I asked her why the leap from Vancouver to Calgary, she noted: "I felt there was an urgency in the sustainable development issues before Calgary and, in particular, with the energy choices before Calgary. This new job allowed me to be at the leading edge on ways to demonstrate that these large entities of significant impact in Alberta could in fact rise up to the challenges of climate change and energy efficiency."

I heard passion in her voice, underlining the word "I felt." In fact, as a gracious changemaker you can see that Coady sees "urgency" as a magic word that helps us open our minds and our doors to social innovation.

She then spoke at length about guiding coalitions, noting "besides getting your own house in order, to make a dent on an issue as significant and complex as lessening our climate impact across Canada, we needed a rainbow coalition, a range of differing organizations and firms that in fact had a common interest around the issue of reducing greenhouse gas emissions." She immediately joined, on coming to Calgary, a set of existing networks, some corporate, some pubic. One example was an existing coalition, started by Suncor Energy, that included Cenovus, Canadian National, and Shell International.

Concessions in Working for a Pipeline Giant

Enbridge's oil pipelines go from the source of the fuel in Alberta through Canadian lands to the users in the United States. So much of her work at Enbridge involved the complex ever-changing competitive pressures for Enbridge to move more aggressively into more natural gas and renewables.

Linda told me that much of the value she brought to Enbridge was the result of her engagement with groups outside the company on climate and energy challenges, matched with her ability to translate what she learned from the outreach into information that could be used in developing a reliable business strategy.

Linda was appointed to represent Enbridge on two special advisory groups established by the governments that gave her another front-row seat on the changing social dynamics. One group advised the government of Alberta; another advised the federal government. The goal was to transition all of Canada into a lower carbon future.

She was one of the executive team that helps Enbridge focus on optimizing current assets as they simultaneously position a growth path involving a range of alternative energy sources.

"From these experiences I was able to bring back two simple but reinforcing pieces of a puzzle back to Enbridge as feedback," she says. "First, it was important to realize that most Canadians believed that reaching a transition involved multiple pathways forward, including energy efficiency, renewable energy, lower carbon oi and gas, and changes in public usage and perception."

During Linda Coady's tenure at Enbridge, the company bought 5 billion dollars of off-shore wind assets in the North Sea of Europe, which was on top of an existing investment of over 5 billion in wind and solar operations in North America itself. "They wanted to see how that shoe of renewables and wind fit." The company's executive team then bought a huge American-based natural gas pipeline infrastructure known as Spectra. These were exciting, Earth-moving decisions.

What did Linda learn during these acquisitions? Again, it was all about recognizing the pattern of human traits for her. "My value was in adding a sense of where the public could embrace us, and *to explain 'a set of immovables'* on climate change and energy issues." If there are many people that have strong opinions on limited information in this world, Linda represents the opposite type of person. Enbridge has expansive information about a range of energy fuels and sources; Linda helped them keep an open mind on how best to operate the world's existing resources.

Besides this openness, Linda learned a second major lesson at Enbridge: being an Enbridge executive cannot be easy.

Considering the size and expense of the ventures they undertake, you'd have to learn to work with a storm of engineers like at Boeing or United Technologies. But then, you'd have to have your goods more out in the face of people. This means your hundreds of lawyers and engineers have to operate, in a sense, in a more public way than, say, Apple, Google, or Facebook (until recently). Not too many people in the public can evaluate an algorithm, its value, or its purpose. Give them a pipeline, and they have many opinions.

It pays to keep in mind why this is special and hard. A single pipeline project from Enbridge, such as the current one under development crossing Canada into America, costs at least 7.5 billion U.S. dollars to build—and engages many thousand landowners and every kind of stakeholder, from environmental to legal to regulatory.

Linda brought in cognitive maps all of these inputs into a coherent internal strategy for the firm. She helped the senior management team blend their internal strategies with public trends and needs. Once again, the magic was discernment of human traits.

Let's pause on a specific case. Enbridge moves a great deal of crude for Suncor Energy, a large Calgary-based firm. Gordon Lambert, a former executive from Suncor, notes, "Linda lives in a loud world, a very loud world. Yet she keeps her hands folded, listening. Energy companies live in what you call, Bruce, 'a swift and severe world.' Yet Linda knows how to quiet the storms, and work toward a social solution."

Although Linda has now retired from Enbridge, her work has helped shape its destiny over the next decade or two. Over the next ten years (2020 to 2030) Enbridge is making major moves in energy transformation. By buying Spectra in the United States, they went from an asset-based company that was 80 percent dependent on shipping petroleum crude to 50 percent crude and 50 percent cleaner and cheaper natural gas. They have spent, during the days of Coady and others, 7.8 billion in renewable assets in North America and Europe, and began asking how they can continue to evolve by 2030 their asset base to one third petroleum, one third natural gas, and one third renewables. This was a massive transformation taking many social skills.

And they did all this a few years before global giants like bp, Delta, and Microsoft began making many commitments to similar goals in a time of this climate crisis.

Over the next ten years (from 2020 to 2030), Enbridge needs a full court press by folks that have the skill set of a Linda Coady—and then some.

The Legacy of Leaders Like Linda Coady

Over decades, whether at the Olympics or at Enbridge, Linda has forced many to rethink what is a social virtue and what is a vice. Functioning at the crosshairs of many social conflicts dominating the news in this 21st century, she remained calm, thoughtful, and supportive.

This contribution to society goes beyond her technical competences. She has demonstrated for many the strong benefits of compliance fundamentals, such as the reduction in fines, the avoidance of penalties, and keeping senior executive time out of court.

She has supplied many decisionmakers with an understandable basis that explains to the public corporate motives to extinguish legal liabilities of the firm. She has displayed an uncanny ability to work with lawyers, engineers, and regulators. Lately, she has helped Enbridge disclose before investors, partners, and advocates how she is helping the company mature their environmental and sustainability performance metrics. All of this has proven invaluable to Canadian society—and to Enbridge.

Yet the deeper legacy of Linda Coady, for me, has to do with her discipline of tracking the fundamentals of human traits.

Why We Lie?

Looking over her long career, I want to explore a concluding feature of her work that causes her conscious distress. She disagrees with the point I made in these two concluding sections; yet in good conscience, I must include them.

She wrote me emphatically once: "Bruce, I do not believe everyone lies. You may believe this. But please associate these statements with yourself and not me." That was plain enough.

One of the core understandings I have, since watching my father die when I was three, is this: Everyone lies. My mother would swear I never saw it. My uncles would tell a different story. It occurred on April Fools' Day too.

In similar fashion, I know many in my firm that hedge when it comes to accuracy, even though I love them and need them. And I can tell you that most bosses' use a type of lying called selective truth. This is even more universally discernible if you recall friends during your University days or the way you behaved on early dates or job interviews. Linda gets uncomfortable whenever these topics come up, insisting, "I am good at helping groups be honest with themselves. I am not good at understanding why people lie."

I disagree.

You may recall that I ended our reflection on the diplomatic skills of Frank Loy with his controlled note about the power in vices. Yet in noting that "everyone lies," I want to come closer to ending the book with something more normal and useful than sophisticated diplomacy.

There are many self-righteous people, and maybe even more isolated people, who claim they never lie. But people like those selected to be featured in this book, to me, seem to understand in quite unique and different ways that all leaders, special interest groups, and people lie to a necessary degree. This makes moving large projects forward, like Vancouver's Olympics or Enbridge's pipelines, even more difficult. Unless you understand why we lie—the Harvard conflict mitigation experts assert—we may remain in an impasse, paralyzing by announced differences.

Now Linda does agree that many people "surround themselves with comfortable truths that reinforce their views of the world." I now believe this may be her concession to my point.

According to the *National Geographic* special from June 2017, "Why We Lie: The Science Behind Our Complicated Relationship with the Truth," there are empirical and survival elements to how and why we lie. They quote the psychologist Bruno Verschuere, when he notes: "The truth comes naturally.... But lying takes effort and a sharp, flexible mind."

This empirical scientific literature—most of it based on medical and military findings—argues that lying is a part of everyone's development process, like walking and talking and interacting with society. Children in all cultures learn how to lie between ages two and five, and when they know, they are ready for either pre-school or kindergarten. This research suggests that lying is both innate and social, a feature of all maturing selves that helps us test our independence as we grow. Review the following image:

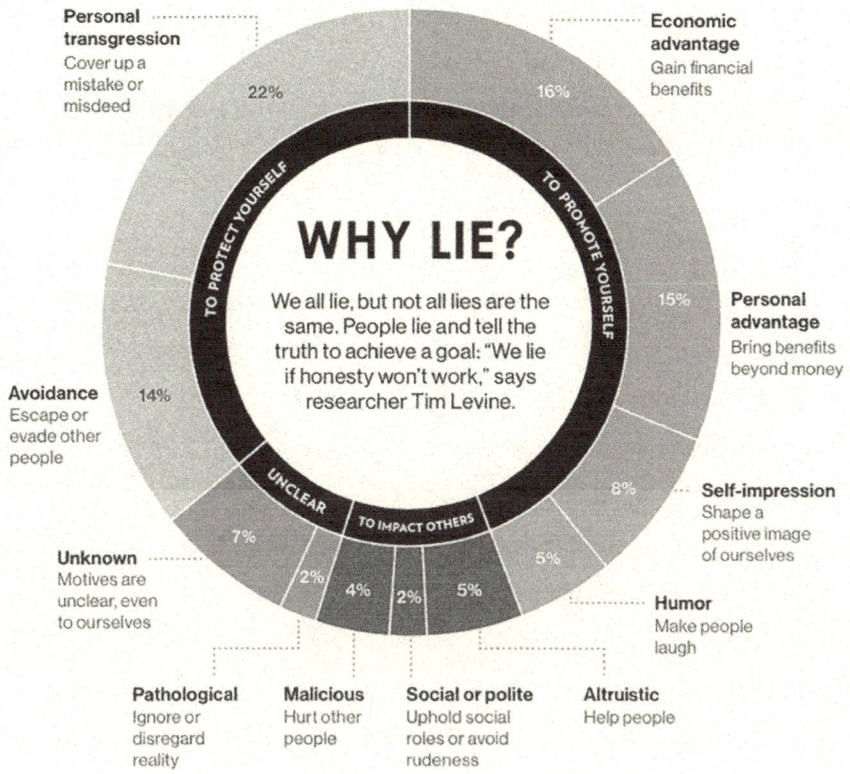

WHY LIE?

We all lie, but not all lies are the same. People lie and tell the truth to achieve a goal: "We lie if honesty won't work," says researcher Tim Levine.

TO PROTECT YOURSELF

TO PROMOTE YOURSELF

TO IMPACT OTHERS

UNCLEAR

Personal transgression 22%
Cover up a mistake or misdeed

Economic advantage 16%
Gain financial benefits

Personal advantage 15%
Bring benefits beyond money

Self-impression 8%
Shape a positive image of ourselves

Humor 5%
Make people laugh

Altruistic 5%
Help people

Social or polite 2%
Uphold social roles or avoid rudeness

Malicious 4%
Hurt other people

Pathological 2%
Ignore or disregard reality

Unknown 7%
Motives are unclear, even to ourselves

Avoidance 14%
Escape or evade other people

Bhattacharjee, Yudhijit (June 2017).
"Why We Lie," *National Geographic*, 231 (6).
Used with permission.

In it you can study—empirically, and connect perhaps with it emotionally—why there are two primary motives to lying: *to protect yourself, or to promote yourself.* Now, it is true that many of the leaders featured in this book appear selfless. I would even assert that most are remarkably selfless. Yet there are more discerning nuances as well.

Looking more closely, *you see that about 22 percent of a person's lies are due to personal transgression*, the need to cover up like a President or a CEO a mistake or a misdeed—in a world moving too fast and seldom beyond blame. I have had direct conversations with Linda

Coady where she is explaining "as context" why this coverup is occurring in a given situation.

When you combine the two major subsets of self-promotion—, economic advantage and personal advantage—you see why people are motivated by social admiration, luxury, and love as much as the strict benefits of money. This will be the final push of examination you will find in our concluding case study of Eileen Fisher. I think her genius is that she knows people want luxury and love and a sense of being in a preferred group more than money.

In Linda's case, she wants resolution, social resolution, more than money. She wants honesty instead of lies.

I believe, despite her proud refusal, that her ability to outsmart the entrenchment of lies in group settings is critical to her legendary success. One of my best graduate students once said, "If we fully understand why people lie, we can learn to balance their self-interests." It is almost as if she keeps that full circle *National Geographic* made in the back of her mind, as she proceeds in addressing a public. Yet she does not need to recognize that she has this in the back of her mind.

Please note this is the opposite of being calculating. She is accepting misperceptions to advance a greater good. *Great facilitators of social needs need to find ways to bracket all human tendencies with respect and impact.* Look around you, Linda Coady suggests.

Is that person an impersonator? Do they have less power than they project, or more, or are they simply trying out a position that they have half certainty in? I am suggesting that it takes a bold self-aware person, with a sense of their own humiliating limits, to become like Linda Coady. Please note her simple honest emphasis here:

*I am not the center of the show. I do not need the
limelight. I like working in the corners to help people
get to the center of things.*

How Does She Do It?

As important as it is to understand what Linda does to analyze
and strategize around people's motives, it's as important to understand
how she does it. For, at the moment, you perhaps visualize her as coldly
observing people, entering her perceptions into a spreadsheet to be
the tabulated expert entrenched parties listen closely to.

But the truth is quite the opposite. She remains part of the fray;
she is in the group; she reflects their humanness. One of the corporate
attorneys that came to my office during my focus group lunch debates
over the cases in this book, James Gamble, asserted when I tried out
these issues: "I like Linda Coady. That is what matters, Bruce. You can
split hairs about what it takes to be like her. The point being is we need
more to be like her. When you are defending a Board from a lawsuit,
as I did for twenty years, you know your goal and you rehearse how to
get there. It strikes me that Linda is likeable because she gives people
a chance to get there together."

Linda called me the other day to say she was taking another "turn"
and had accepted a job as the Executive Director of a major Canadian
environmental think tank on climate and energy issues, this at age
of 68. What this means is as this book comes out, she will be very
much in the fray. In addition, she is taking a role to serve the Prime
Minister of Canada on a very direct and difficult public dispute. All
I can say is this takes gusto, focus, an ability that navigates a world
of lies, and a gift of deep listening.

Chapter Snapshot:
Linda Coady

- Humility and civility in purpose
- Strategic and social with the ability and willingness to listen
- Quiet wit, with abundant action
- Consistently working a social purpose for social good

Afterword
by Darryl Poole

In Bruce Piasecki's exceptional 2007 book, *World, Inc.*, he wrote that "this book...identifies a pattern within capitalism that is larger than any specific example of good corporate leadership. It offers lasting concepts on how, within society itself, there are forces that are pushing capitalism into new forms and responsibilities." At the same time, in his management consulting work, Bruce began to expand discussions of corporate social responsibility to embrace the more pressing global problems of business growth and sustainability.

Bruce's next three books—*Doing More with Less: The New Way to Wealth* (2012), *Doing More with Teams: The New Way to Winning* (2014), and *New World Companies: The Future of Capitalism* (2016)—reflected the evolution of his management practice, from tactical planning to team management to the identification and delivery of world-class corporate performance.

Now comes a very different book: a study of six accomplished people who are purpose-driven, selfless, and deeply reflective. Through carefully wrought portraits, both intimate and evocative, Bruce depicts exceptional leaders, each with a unique blend of character and skill. Through these character studies, Bruce suggests how and why some firms succeed while others falter, by linking organizational achievement to the personalities of those who drive it.

In this book, Bruce explores the realm of leadership by life example. He does so by illuminating the lives of men and women whose influence extends far beyond their own firms—embracing staff, colleagues, customers, governments, and even markets. Thousands have been impacted, not only by what these leaders have done, but by how they have lived. Their example offers a message to all of us: we are often better than we realize. And, should we choose to embrace it, faith in who we are, and faith in others, often carries more weight than the entities we choose to serve.

This is the right time for such a book. First, these six lives exemplify the lessons of Julie Benezet's 2016 book, *The Journey of Not Knowing: How 21st-Century Leaders Can Chart a Course Where There Is None*, which explores the challenges of leading firms across uncharted territory and offers guidance on how to meet those challenges.

This new Piasecki book reveals not only how these men and women have succeeded, but what it takes. As Bruce writes, his subjects have mastered the art of "advancing with dignity and result." All share five essential traits: uncompromising ethics, gifted dedication, compassionate insight, focused reflection, and uncommon civility. Bruce offers us a uniquely personal perspective on the lives of leaders who are human—just like you and me—people whose lives we may have been curious about but never had the opportunity to see.

I predict this book will take its place among important readings in social biography, along with *The Wise Men: Six Friends and the World They Made* (Walter Isaacson and Evan Thomas, 1986), *Mirror to America: The Autobiography of John Hope Franklin* (2005), *Consider: Harnessing the Power of Reflective Thinking in Your Organization* (Daniel Patrick Forrester, 2011), *The Quartet: Orchestrating the Second*

American Revolution, 1783–1789 (Joseph J. Ellis, 2015), and *Jewish Justices of the Supreme Court: From Brandeis to Kagan* (David G. Dalin, 2017). As different as these books are, each offers a window into the minds of remarkable individuals who were at the center of complex and critical change.

As to who they are in our own subjective mirrors, these six are people who are often lost in histories dominated by either selfless circumstance, crises, and/or self-aggrandizing personalities who encourage their own cults.

Four of the six portraits incorporate a number of additional characters beyond the principal subjects. The resulting shifts in focus yield essential context that could not have been communicated without such a kaleidoscopic—if occasionally dizzying—view. The Eileen Fisher chapter is emotively and cerebrally as stunning as the Frank Loy chapter. In the latter there is brilliance. In the former there is genius.

Bruce is an accomplished advocate of conscious and socially balanced investment within a framework of clarity rather than charity; of sustainable, long-term yields rather than short-term gains. In his view, personal success is not enough: we must lead others to success. And to do that, we must understand why we lead, and what is required of those whom we trust to lead.

A practitioner and facilitator as well as a close observer of executive behaviors, Bruce continues to evolve as a social historian, futurist, and strategist, combining the prescience and narrative skill of Joseph M. Juran, Peter Drucker, Carmen Reihart, Kenneth Rogoff, and John Hope Franklin. Every chapter resonates with keenly applied and compassionate intelligence.

While the fluid prose of this book lends itself to a quick, comfortable read, the sensitive, nuanced portraits are unlike anything else readers are likely to have encountered. As such, they are meant to be savored. Because of its depth and extraordinary insight, this is not a book for the faint of heart: it will challenge readers at a deep level—particularly those who see themselves as already "successful." By revealing what these six leaders have experienced, what they think and feel, what they do—and, most important, how they have made their mark on the world—Bruce compels us to explore and perhaps redefine our vision of what constitutes success.

As a pragmatic ethicist with a background in finance, I see *Conquering Tomorrow Today* as a fitting guide for taxed executives and driven professionals, offering a vision of how to choose to be what you truly are, by discovering that you have more innate courage than you may believe. The narratives of shared ethical accomplishment may be an "easy read," but they trace the twists and turns of a tough life mission.

D.V. Poole
Private Executive Advisory

Reflections on Personality and Social Cohesion

In this bio-sketch series, you meet six of the world's most extraordinary personalities—down to earth and humble people who have redefined what it means to succeed in business and excel in society. For decades, they have navigated through the world's largest corporations and powerful governments, redirecting how these giants operate and impact the world. And, most likely, you have never heard their names before.

Why write biographies of people who are largely unknown? I've been asked this question countless times: by friends, family, editors, and colleagues; and even by the very people profiled in this book.

Here is a reason:

These six personality types have proven prescient on how to compete in today's swift and severe world. In addition, these six people offer you a way to make your own life more consequential.

* * * * *

I have read books like this before.

I remember from college, vividly, Vasari's book on *Italian Painters*, where you got a glimpse of the essence of the painters in action. Then, during graduate studies, there was Sigmund Freud's early case study work; and then, in the last decade, my favorite by far, Winston Churchill's colorful account of his acquaintances in *Great Contemporaries*. In this collection, Winston Churchill brought alive personalities such as Lawrence of Arabia long before anyone knew of them.

These interesting short biographies are not written with monumental detail. This is a compositional choice I made, to be sure to get you a sampling of six rather than death by historic details on one. At times, for certain biographies, the reader needs a depth of detail. I think back and celebrate how William Manchester wrote on Churchill himself, or how Ron Chernow wrote about Alexander Hamilton or when Robert Caro spent a life in pursuit of L.B. Johnson or Taylor Branch recreating the 100 preachers before he gets to Martin Luther King. My bet, in today's swift and severe world, is that people who want to fix the world want more urgency in profiles.

That is why we offer you here short, lively accounts of the essence of individual you'd find curious. While perfectly ordinary people in many respects, they are given force and gravity by society. And it is preciously through their personalities that they inspire loyalty, respect, and one of the rarest remaining social amenities of today: social cohesion.

*　*　*　*　*

Let me explain what I mean by social cohesion.

These personalities are gifted at making the patterns of today meaningful and believable rather than confused. Instead of gaining strength through turmoil and distrust, they help society cohere. There is a stunning coherence in what they do. We need them today in our most turbulent world more than ever. Our world filled with police brutality, carbon and capital constraints, and constant political bickering seems beyond calm, beyond resolution. Until you watch what these lives do.

Dacher Kellner gets to the core of what makes these lives matter in this opening passage to his book, *The Power Paradox*:

> *"Life is made up of patterns. Patterns of eating, thirst, sleep, and fight or flight are crucial to our individual survival; patterns of courtship, sex, attachment, conflict, play, creativity, family life, and collaboration are crucial to our collective survival.* Wisdom *is our ability to perceive these patterns and to shape them into* coherent chapters *within the longer narrative of our lives. In this way, wisdom survives crisis. That is what is needed this decade, and those decades ahead."*

Yes, we can say the six I've chosen to spend three years writing about constitute acts of wisdom. That is what I am dramatizing here— their state of wisdom. I am not offering exactly how they won a case or made a business decision. I provide essential sketches, not exhaustive how-to learning here, for I do not really believe what the future needs is more manuals. What the future needs is the cultivation of the skills you can glean from meeting these six. You may be malicious, you may be altruistic, you may be neither. What matters is how effective you can become in line with the principles found in their lives.

Like surfers in a lasting storm, these six business and social leaders know *why they are out there.* Their lives have proven meaningful to far more than themselves, their families, and their friends. I ask, "How did that happen?"

Bruce Piasecki,
Saratoga Springs, New York
Summer of 2020
(written after a month of racial tensions exploded by the death of George Floyd)

Full Book Table of Contents

(Available 2021)

Foreword
By **Chris Coulter, CEO, GlobeScan** 5

Chapter One
What is Enough? 15

Chapter Two
Why Some Are Noble: Frank Loy 18

Chapter Three
What Money Enables: John Streur 54

Chapter Four
The Social Intelligence of Linda Coady 83

Chapter Five
Why We Adventure: Steve Percy 130

Chapter Six
Like a Rock of Dignity: Jackson Robinson 171

Chapter Seven
The Quiet Genius of Eileen Fisher 200

Afterword, by **Darryl Poole** 245

The Conversation:
About Bruce Piasecki

How is corporate America responding to the global COVID-19 outbreak and how are major multi-national corporations dealing with ongoing global issues such as climate change and economic inequality?

We spoke with best-selling business author and management consultant **Bruce Piasecki** to learn about the economic impact of the coronavirus pandemic on global corporations and how they are responding to the ongoing challenges.

In addition to being a sought-after speaker and leading management consultant, Dr. Piasecki is a best-selling author of a dozen books, including *Doing More With Less: The New Way to Wealth*; *Doing More With Teams: The New Way to Winning*; *New World Companies: The Future of Capitalism*; and *World, Inc.*, which has been published in 10 foreign editions and has won several awards on globalization. In addition to his business books, Dr. Piasecki also wrote a memoir, *Missing Persons: A Life of Unexpected Influences*, which includes a foreword by author Jay Parini.

Dr. Piasecki earned his Bachelor's and Ph.D. degrees from Cornell University and has run professional education and degree programs at Cornell, Clarkson University, and Rensselaer Polytechnic University.

At RPI, he developed one of the nation's first Master of Science degree programs in Environmental Management and Policy.

Watch the Paul Grondahl/Dr. Bruce Piasecki interview at *The Conversation*: https://www.nyswritersinstitute.org/post/the-economic-impact-of-the-pandemic-on-global-corporations